POP MUSIC 1960S-2000S

CHRISTMAS
QUIZ BOOK

FOR ALL THE FAMILY

HOW WELL DO YOU KNOW 1960S MUSIC?

1960s QUIZ 1

Q1: IS PENNY LANE NAMED AFTER A STREET IN LONDON, LIVERPOOL OR LUTON?

Q2: WHO IS THE LEAD SINGER OF THE ROLLING STONES?

Q3: WHAT WAS ELVIS PRESLEY'S FIRST NUMBER ONE HIT OF THE 1960S?

Q4: WHICH 1960S BOND FILM DID TOM JONES SING THE TITLE TRACK FOR?

Q5: WHO WAS THE ENGLISH MEMBER OF THE 1960S BAND 'THE MONKEES'?

Q6: WHAT KIND OF PLANE WERE PETER PAUL AND MARY LEAVING ON?

Q7: WHAT JOB DID LONNIE DONEGAN'S OLD MAN HAVE IN HIS MARCH 1960 HIT SONG?

Q8: WHICH EMOTION DID KEN DODD SING ABOUT IN 1964?

Q9: THE MOODY BLUES FORMED IN WHICH BRITISH CITY IN 1964?

Q10: 'IT'S NOT UNUSUAL' WAS THE FIRST NUMBER ONE HIT IN 1965 FOR WHICH WELSH SINGER?

Q11: WHEN DID 'TOP OF THE POPS' FIRST APPEAR ON OUR TV SCREENS?

Q12: BRYAN HYLAND SANG ABOUT WHAT TYPE OF 'YELLOW POLKADOT BIKINI' IN JUNE 1960?

Q13: THE NAMES OF TWO BLUES MUSICIANS, PINK ANDERSON AND FLOYD COUNCIL, GAVE SID BARRETT THE NAME FOR WHICH BAND?

Q14: WHAT WAS CILLA BLACK'S FIRST NUMBER 1 HIT IN FEBRUARY 1964?

Q15: RICHIE HAVENS SANG THE OPENING SONG AT WHICH FAMOUS MUSIC FESTIVAL ON 15TH AUGUST 1969?

Q16: WHO WAS THE LEAD SINGER OF THE DOORS, FOUNDED IN 1965?

Q17: WHICH BAND SANG 'CALIFORNIA DREAMIN'', RELEASED ON 8TH DECEMBER 1965?

Q18: HOW MANY UK NUMBER 1S DID THE BEATLES HAVE IN THE 1960S?

Q19: WHAT COLOUR WAS THE ROLLING STONES 'PAINTING IT' IN MAY 1966?

Q20: WHOSE DEBUT ALBUM WAS CALLED 'HELLO, I'M DOLLY' IN 1967?

HOW WELL ARE YOU DOING SO FAR?

Q1: WHO WERE MANFRED MANN'S 2 LEAD VOCALISTS?

Q2: WHICH BRITISH BAND PERFORMED LIVE ON THE ED SULLIVAN SHOW ON FEBRUARY 9TH 1964?

Q3: WHICH FAMOUS GUITARIST FORMED THE BAND CREAM WITH GINGER BAKER AND JACK BRUCE IN 1966?

Q4: WHICH BAND HAD A NUMBER 1 HIT WITH 'YOU'LL NEVER WALK ALONE' IN 1963?

Q5: WHAT SHADE OF PALE DID THE ENGLISH ROCK BAND PROCUL HAREM SING ABOUT IN 1967?

1960s QUIZ 2

Q6: 'YOU CAN'T HURRY LOVE' WAS A HIT FOR WHICH MOTOWN BAND IN JULY 1966?

Q7: WHICH ERIC BURDON BAND WAS FORMED IN NEWCASTLE UPON TYNE IN THE EARLY 1960S?

Q8: WHAT SONG WAS THE LAST UK NUMBER 1 FOR THE BEATLES?

Q9: WHERE WAS THE DAKOTAS SINGER, BILLY J KRAMER, BORN?

Q10: ON WHICH 1967 BEATLES ALBUM WILL YOU FIND 'A LITTLE HELP FROM MY FRIENDS'?

1960s QUIZ 2

Q11: WHO WAS YODELLING FRANK IFIELD REMEMBERING IN 1962?

Q12: WHICH SONGS WERE NUMBER 1 HITS FOR TOM JONES IN THE 1960S?

Q13: APACHE TOPPED THE SINGLES CHART FOR 5 WEEKS IN 1960 FOR WHICH BAND?

Q14: THE THEME SONG FROM THE 1967 FILM 'TO SIR WITH LOVE' WAS A HIT FOR WHICH SINGER?

Q15: WHAT IS THE FIRST LINE OF THE SONG 'BLOWIN IN THE WIND' BY BOB DYLAN?

Q16: WHAT WAS 'OVER' FOR THE SEEKERS IN THEIR 1965 HIT?

Q17: WHO SANG CHART TOPPING SINGLES 'RELEASE ME' AND 'THE LAST WALTZ' IN 1967?

Q18: WHAT WAS SANDIE SHAW'S 3RD NUMBER 1 HIT IN 1967?

Q19: WHICH BAND HAD ITS FIRST UK NUMBER 1 HIT WITH 'IT'S ALL OVER NOW' IN JULY 1964?

Q20: WHICH AMERICAN SINGER WAS THE FINAL PERFORMER AT THE WOODSTOCK FESTIVAL IN 1969?

HOW WELL DO YOU KNOW 1970S MUSIC?

1970S QUIZ 1

Q1: WHO GOT CAUGHT IN THE RAIN WITH A PINA COLADA IN HIS 1979 HIT?

Q2: THE BEATLES RELEASED THEIR FINAL ALBUM IN MAY OF WHICH YEAR?

Q3: WHO WAS THE LEAD SINGER OF HOT CHOCOLATE?

Q4: LULU SANG THE TITLE SONG OF WHICH 1970S BOND MOVIE?

Q5: THE BOYS ARE BACK WHERE, IN THE THIN LIZZY SONG?

Q6: WHAT WAS THE NAME OF SIMON AND GARFUNKEL'S FINAL ALBUM?

Q7: WHAT COLOUR LADY DID DAVID SOUL SING ABOUT IN 1977?

Q8: ZIGGY STARDUST WAS THE FLAMBOYANT ALTER EGO OF WHICH SINGER?

Q9: WHAT YEAR DID THE SONY WALKMAN ENABLE US TO LISTEN ON THE GO?

Q10: WHICH YEAR DID ABBA WIN THE EUROVISION SONG CONTEST?

1970s
QUIZ
1

Q11: WHAT SONG DOES 'WELL YOU CAN TELL BY THE WAY I USE MY WALK...' COME FROM?

Q12: WHAT WAS THE BEST SELLING SINGLE OF THE 1970S?

Q13: WHICH BAND RELEASED 'THE SONGS REMAIN THE SAME' LIVE ALBUM IN 1976?

Q14: WHAT WAS THE BEST-SELLING FILM SOUNDTRACK ALBUM OF THE 1970S?

Q15: WHO ASKED THE QUESTION: 'ARE FRIENDS ELECTRIC?' IN 1979?

Q16: WHAT DOES ELTON JOHN SAY IS THE HARDEST WORD?

Q17: HARRY WAYNE CASEY IS THE KC IN WHICH BAND?

Q18: 'YOU'RE THE ONE THAT I WANT' COMES FROM WHICH 1970S FILM?

Q19: WHICH ALBUM WOULD YOU FIND FLEETWOOD MAC'S 'YOU MAKE LOVIN' FUN'?

Q20: WHICH BAND DID ROY WOOD LEAVE TO FORM WIZZARD IN JULY 1972?

HOW WELL ARE YOU DOING SO FAR?

Q1: The name of Ray Dorset's band 'Mungo Jerry' was inspired by a poem from which writer's 'Old Possum's Book of Practical Cats'?

Q2: What song did Mary Hopkin sing as the UK entry for the 1970 Eurovision Song Contest?

Q3: Wild Cherry, American funk rock band, is most famous for which song?

Q4: In 1961 the Marvelettes sang 'Please Mr Postman' but who band sang it in 1975?

Q5: How many weeks did 'You're The One That I Want' sung by Olivia Newton John and John Travolta top in the UK charts in 1978?

1970s QUIZ 2

Q6: WHICH SONG WAS THE BAY CITY ROLLERS' FIRST NUMBER 1 HIT IN MARCH 1975?

Q7: IN WHAT YEAR DID THE WHO RELEASE THE ALBUM QUADROPHENIA?

Q8: IN JULY 1975 THE STYLISTICS HAD A NUMBER 1 HIT WITH WHICH SONG?

Q9: IN WHAT YEAR DID THE COMMODORES RELEASE 'YOU'RE THREE TIMES A LADY'?

Q10: WHICH BAND WON EUROVISION FOR THE UK WITH 'SAVE YOUR KISSES FOR ME' IN 1976?

Q11: WHO DID ELTON JOHN DUET WITH IN HIS 1976 SONG 'DON'T GO BREAKING MY HEART'?

Q12: WHAT WAS DAVID BOWIE'S BACKING BAND CALLED IN THE EARLY 1970S?

Q13: IN KATE BUSH'S 1978 SONG, WHAT DID THE MAN HAVE IN HIS EYES?

Q14: WHAT DID MARVIN GAYE WANT YOU TO SEE IN HIS 1971 SONG?

Q15: IN MAY 1973 TUBULAR BELLS WAS THE DEBUT ALBUM FOR WHICH ENGLISH MUSICIAN AND COMPOSER?

1970s QUIZ 2

Q16: WHAT KIND OF FIGHTING DID CARL DOUGLAS SING ABOUT IN 1974?

Q17: WHICH COUNTRIES THREATENED TO THROW OUT DAVID CASSIDY ON HIS 1974 TOUR DUE TO THE MASS HYSTERIA OF HIS FANS?

Q18: WHICH EX BEATLE HAD THE FIRST SOLO NUMBER 1 IN 1970?

Q19: THE 1976 SONG 'THE COMBINE HARVESTER' WAS A NUMBER 1 HIT FOR WHICH BAND?

Q20: MICK JAGGER SANG BACKING VOCALS FOR WHICH 1973 CARLY SIMON SONG?

1980s

QuIZ

1

HOW WELL DO YOU KNOW 1980S MuSIC?

Q1: WHICH BAND PLAYED THE OPENING SONG FOR LIVE AID AT WEMBLEY STADIUM ON JULY 13TH 1985?

Q2: ALL CRIED OUT CAME FROM WHICH 1984 ALISON MOYET ALBUM?

Q3: BACK IN BLACK WAS A 1980 ALBUM FOR WHICH BAND?

Q4: A-HA SANG THE TITLE TRACK FOR WHICH 1980S BOND FILM?

Q5: WHICH SOAP OPERA DID QUEEN PARODY WITH 'I WANT TO BREAK FREE' IN 1984?

Q6: NEVER GONNA GIVE YOU UP WAS A 1987 HIT FOR WHICH SINGER?

Q7: IN WHICH YEAR DID WHITNEY HOUSTON SING 'SAVING ALL MY LOVE FOR YOU'?

Q8: WHO SANG THE FIRST LINE OF THE 1984 VERSION OF DO THEY KNOW IT'S CHRISTMAS?

Q9: IN 1987 THE PROCLAIMERS WERE WAITING FOR A LETTER FROM WHERE?

Q10: ADAM AND THE ANTS HAD A NUMBER 1 IN 1981 WITH WHICH SONG?

1980s QUIZ 1

Q11: THERE'S NO ONE QUITE LIKE GRANDMA WAS A CHRISTMAS NUMBER 1 IN 1980 FOR WHO?

Q12: ROBERT DE NIRO WAS WAITING FOR WHICH BAND IN 1984?

Q13: WHAT WAS THE NAME OF THE BAND WHO WON THE EUROVISION SONG CONTEST IN 1981 WITH 'MAKING YOUR MIND UP'?

Q14: WHERE DID GEORGE MICHAEL FIRST MEET ANDREW RIDGELEY?

Q15: WHICH GROUP RELEASED THE JOSHUA TREE ALBUM IN 1987?

1980s
QUIZ
1

Q16: THE SIMPLE MINDS' SONG 'DON'T YOU (FORGET ABOUT ME)' WAS PLAYED IN THE CREDITS OF WHICH 1985 AMERICAN TEEN COMEDY DRAMA?

Q17: WHICH AMERICAN BAND SANG 'DON'T STOP BELIEVIN'' IN 1981?

Q18: WHAT DID TOTO BLESS IN THEIR 1982 SONG AFRICA?

Q19: WHICH IRISH SINGER-SONGWRITER'S REAL NAME IS PAUL DAVID HEWSON?

Q20: WHO SANG 'THE ONLY WAY IS UP' IN 1980?

1980s QUIZ 2

HOW WELL ARE YOU DOING SO FAR?

Q1: WHICH SONG DID THE AMERICAN ROCK BAND SURVIVOR, RELEASE IN MAY 1982?

Q2: WHICH BAND DID CHRISTOPHER HAMILL BECOME THE NEW LEAD SINGER FOR IN 1981?

Q3: WHAT SONG BECAME A UK NUMBER 1 FOR MUSICAL YOUTH IN OCTOBER 1982?

Q4: THE FILM DESPERATELY SEEKING SUSAN, FEATURED WHICH MADONNA SONG IN 1985?

Q5: NEW EDITION SANG 'CANDY GIRL' IN WHICH YEAR?

Q6: WHO ARE THE BAND MEMBERS OF THE PET SHOP BOYS FORMED IN 1981?

Q7: WHO SANG 'JAPANESE BOY', IN 1981?

Q8: MEL AND KIM REACHED NUMBER 1 IN THE UK IN 1987 WITH WHICH SONG?

Q9: ARETHA FRANKLIN SANG A DUET WITH WHICH ENGLISH SINGER IN 1987?

Q10: BARBARA GASKIN AND DAVE STEWART SANG A COVER VERSION OF WHICH SONG IN 1981?

Q11: Tiffany sang 'I Think We're Alone Now' in 1987. What is Tiffany's surname?

Q12: The Fairytale of New York missed out on a Christmas number 1 in 1987 because of which song by The Pet Shop Boys?

Q13: Which ska revival band had a number 1 hit with 'Ghost Town' in 1981?

Q14: Dexys Midnight Runners sang 'Come On Eileen' in which year?

Q15: ABBA sang 'Super Trouper' in November 1980, but what is a Super Trouper?

1980s QUIZ 2

Q16: KEEP YOUR DISTANCE WAS THE DEBUT ALBUM FOR WHICH BAND IN 1987?

Q17: WHICH SONG BECAME A UK NUMBER 1 IN MARCH 1988 FOR ASWAD?

Q18: LED ZEPPELIN'S DRUMMER DIED IN 1980. WHO WAS HE?

Q19: WHAT BAND DID DAVE HEATON FORM AFTER THE BREAKUP OF THE HOUSEMARTINS IN 1988?

Q20: WHAT SONG WAS THE ONLY UK NUMBER 1 FOR BROS?

1990s

QUIZ

1

HOW WELL DO YOU KNOW 1990S MUSIC?

1990s
QUIZ
1

Q1: WHICH ACTOR NARRATED SOME OF THE WORDS IN BLUR'S 1994 SONG PARKLIFE?

Q2: '...BABY ONE MORE TIME', RELEASED IN 1998, WAS THE FIRST SINGLE FOR WHICH ARTIST?

Q3: WHAT IS THE NAME OF OASIS' SECOND STUDIO ALBUM, RELEASED IN OCTOBER 1995?

Q4: WHO IS THE OLDEST MEMBER OF TAKE THAT?

Q5: WHICH BAND IS MISSING FROM THE BRITPOP 'BIG FOUR' OASIS, BLUR, PULP?

Q6: WHICH SONG REACHED NUMBER 2 IN THE UK CHARTS IN JUNE 1997 FOR THE VERVE?

Q7: MIAMI 7 WAS THE CHILDREN'S SERIES THAT WHICH BAND FIRST APPEARED ON?

Q8: MADONNA'S 1990 SINGLE 'VOGUE' WAS RELEASED FROM WHICH ALBUM?

Q9: IN WHICH YEAR DID KURT COBAIN FROM NIRVANA DIE?

Q10: WHICH BAND HAD A HIT WITH 'LOSING MY RELIGION' IN 1991?

1990S QUIZ 1

Q11: WHICH WHITNEY HOUSTON SONG BECAME A HIT AFTER FIRST BEING HEARD IN THE FILM THE BODYGUARD?

Q12: NATALIE IMBRUGLIA WAS A REGULAR IN WHICH AUSTRALIAN SOAP OPERA?

Q13: WHO WAS NOTHING COMPARES 2 U A CHART HIT FOR IN 1990?

Q14: JOHN SQUIRE WAS THE LEAD GUITARIST FOR WHICH BAND?

Q15: IN WHAT YEAR WAS 'SIT DOWN' BY MANCHESTER ALTERNATIVE ROCK BAND JAMES RELEASED?

Q16: The 1991 Bryan Adams song, (Everything I Do) I Do It For You was featured in which film?

Q17: Free As A Bird was released in 1995 and sung by members of which band that had stopped performing 25 years before?

Q18: When was the American vocal group the Backstreet Boys formed?

Q19: Eddie Vedder is the lead singer with which American rock band, formed in Seattle in 1990?

Q20: What was English alternative rock band Radiohead's debut single, released in September 1992?

HOW WELL ARE YOU DOING SO FAR?

1990s QUIZ 2

Q1: BRITISH SYNTH-POP DUO ERASURE RELEASED AN EP IN JUNE 1992 AS A TRIBUTE TO WHICH BAND?

Q2: STARS WAS A BEST-SELLING UK ALBUM OF THE YEAR FOR 1991 AND 1992 FOR WHICH BAND?

Q3: STAY BY SHAKESPEARE SISTER WAS RELEASED IN JANUARY 1992 AND TOPPED THE UK SINGLES CHARTS FOR HOW MANY CONSECUTIVE WEEKS?

Q4: WHAT IS BRITISH SINGER-SONGWRITER GABRIELLE'S FIRST NAME?

Q5: WHAT YEAR DID GERRI HALLIWELL LEAVE THE SPICE GIRLS?

1990s QUIZ 2

Q6: DANISH SINGER WHIGFIELD SANG ABOUT WHICH NIGHT IN HER 1994 SINGLE?

Q7: WHO WROTE SINEAD O'CONNOR'S 1990 HIT SINGLE NOTHING COMPARES 2 U?

Q8: WHICH BRITPOP SINGER CREATED A DISTURBANCE DURING MICHAEL JACKSON'S PERFORMANCE OF EARTHSONG IN THE 1996 BRIT AWARDS?

Q9: WHAT WAS BLUR'S FIRST NUMBER 1 SINGLE IN 1995?

Q10: WHICH GEORGE MICHAEL SONG DID ROBBIE WILLIAMS COVER TO LAUNCH HIS SOLO CAREER IN 1996?

1990s QUIZ 2

Q11: WHICH ENGLISH ROCK BAND FORMED IN SALFORD BROKE UP FOR THE FIRST TIME IN 1992?

Q12: POPMART WAS A BEST-SELLING TOUR IN 1997 FOR WHICH BAND?

Q13: WHO PLAYED GUITAR FOR THE RED HOT CHILLI PEPPERS' 1995 ALBUM ONE HOT MINUTE?

Q14: WHAT YEAR WAS THE CHILDREN IN NEED VERSION OF LOU REED'S SONG PERFECT DAY RELEASED?

Q15: WHICH CHER SINGLE WAS ONE OF THE TOP BEST-SELLING OF ALL TIME?

1990s QUIZ 2

Q16: WHAT WAS JIMMY NAIL'S MOST SUCCESSFUL WORLDWIDE HIT RELEASED IN 1992?

Q17: WHICH DANISH DANCE POP GROUP SANG BARBIE GIRL IN 1997?

Q18: BETTER THE DEVIL YOU KNOW RELEASED IN APRIL 1990 IS DESCRIBED AS THE REINVENTION SINGLE FOR WHICH ARTIST?

Q19: VIRTUAL INSANITY WAS RELEASED IN AUGUST 1996 BY WHICH BRITISH FUNK BAND?

Q20: NORMAN QUENTIN COOK IS THE REAL NAME OF WHICH ENGLISH MUSICIAN, DJ AND RECORD PRODUCER?

2000s

QUIZ

1

HOW WELL DO YOU KNOW 2000S MUSIC?

2000s QUIZ 1

Q1: WHICH SINGLE WENT STRAIGHT TO NUMBER 1 IN 2002 FOR WILL YOUNG?

Q2: WHICH SINGLE WAS A CHRISTMAS NUMBER 1 IN 2008 FOR ALEXANDRA BURKE?

Q3: WHICH CHART-TOPPING SINGLE IN 2007 EARNED RHIANNA HER FIRST GRAMMY AWARD?

Q4: STEFANI JOANNE ANGELINA GERMANOTTA IS THE REAL NAME OF WHICH AMERICAN SINGER, SONGWRITER AND ACTOR?

Q5: WHAT WAS THE NAME OF BEYONCE'S FIRST SOLO ALBUM IN 2003 DURING DESTINY'S CHILD'S BREAK FROM PERFORMING?

2000s QUIZ 1

Q6: WHICH BLACK EYED PEAS SONG WENT ON TO BECOME BRITAIN'S BEST SELLING SINGLE OF 2003?

Q7: MARSHALL BRUCE MATHERS III IS KNOWN PROFESSIONALLY AS WHO?

Q8: AFTER RELEASING HIS FIRST STUDIO ALBUM, LIFE IN CARTOON MOTION, WHO WON A BEST BRITISH BREAKTHROUGH ACT BRIT AWARD IN 2008?

Q9: WHAT DID ENGLISH INDIE ROCK BAND KAISER CHIEFS ORIGINALLY CALL THEMSELVES IN 2000?

Q10: WHAT IS THE SURNAME OF ALL FOUR MEMBERS OF THE AMERICAN ROCK BAND KINGS OF LEON?

2000s QUIZ 1

Q11: IN WHAT YEAR DID 'PATIENCE' HELP TAKE THAT MAKE A COMEBACK?

Q12: WHAT IS THE NAME OF AMERICAN ROCK BAND THE KILLERS SECOND STUDIO ALBUM, RELEASED IN 2006?

Q13: SCOTTISH SINGER-SONGWRITER EMELI SANDE RELEASED WHICH ALBUM IN FEBRUARY 2012

Q14: WHO SANG I KISSED A GIRL IN 2008?

Q15: BOB THE BUILDER BEAT WHICH IRISH BOY BAND TO THE CHRISTMAS NUMBER 1 SLOT IN 2000?

Q16: THE ENGLISH ROCK BAND, ARCTIC MONKEYS, WAS FORMED IN WHICH ENGLISH CITY IN 2002?

Q17: WHAT PROFESSIONAL NAME IS THE AMERICAN RAPPER, SHAWN COREY CARTER, KNOWN AS?

Q18: WHICH AMERICAN RAPPER WAS GIVEN HIS STAR ON THE HOLLYWOOD WALK OF FAME IN NOVEMBER 2018?

Q19: IN WHICH YEAR DID SCOTTISH SINGER SUSAN BOYLE WIN BRITAIN'S GOT TALENT?

Q20: WHICH MANCHESTER SOUL AND POP BAND RELEASED A COVER OF THE STYLISTICS' 'YOU MAKE ME FEEL BRAND NEW' IN THEIR ALBUM HOME IN MARCH 2003?

2000s QUIZ 2

HOW WELL ARE YOU DOING SO FAR?

Q1: WHICH AMERICAN SINGER-SONGWRITER RELEASED HER EPONYMOUS DEBUT STUDIO ALBUM IN 2006?

Q2: WHICH SONG DID ENGLISH-IRISH POP GIRL GROUP, GIRLS ALOUD, WIN A 2009 BRIT AWARD FOR BEST SINGLE?

Q3: WHAT WAS THE NAME OF THE SUPERGROUP BUSTED FORMED WITH MCFLY IN 2013?

Q4: WHAT WAS THE NAME OF LIBERTY X'S DEBUT ALBUM, RELEASED IN MAY 2002?

Q5: AMERICAN SINGER-SONGWRITER AND ACTOR, KELLY ROWLAND, WAS A JUDGE ON WHICH TALENT SHOW IN THE UK IN 2011?

2000s QUIZ 2

Q6: PCD, RELEASED IN 2005, WAS THE MULTI-PLATINUM DEBUT ALBUM FOR WHICH AMERICAN GIRL GROUP?

Q7: WHICH YEAR DID LEONA LEWIS WIN X FACTOR?

Q8: WHICH COLUMBIAN SINGER-SONGWRITER HAS ALSO BEEN KNOWN AS LA SHAK AND SHAKI?

Q9: WELSH TENOR, PAUL POTTS, WON BRITAIN'S GOT TALENT 2007 WITH WHICH ARIA FROM PUCCINI'S TURANDOT?

Q10: WHICH SONG DID TAKE THAT PERFORM AT THE LONDON 2012 OLYMPIC GAMES CLOSING CEREMONY?

2000s QUIZ 2

Q11: WHO DID ROBBIE WILLIAMS SING SOMETHIN' STUPID WITH CHRISTMAS 2001?

Q12: RED GIRL RECORDS, FOUNDED IN 2004, IS THE RECORD COMPANY OF WHICH SPICE GIRL WHO BEGAN HER SOLO CAREER WITH A DUET WITH BRYAN ADAMS?

Q13: WHICH DIANA ROSS SONG, RELEASED IN 1993, DID BRITISH POP GROUP, STEPS, COVER IN 2001?

Q14: WHAT IS THE NAME OF BRITNEY SPEARS 2ND ALBUM RELEASED IN 2000?

Q15: RELEASED IN MAY 2007, WHAT WAS MAROON 5'S SECOND ALBUM CALLED?

2000s QUIZ 2

Q16: WHICH BRITISH GIRL GROUP WON THE X FACTOR IN 2011?

Q17: WHO DID RITA ORA REPLACE WHEN SHE BECAME A COACH ON THE FOURTH SERIES OF THE VOICE IN 2015?

Q18: WHICH SCOTTISH INDIE ROCK BAND WANTED TO 'TAKE ME OUT' IN 2004?

Q19: EVERYDAY LIFE IS AN ALBUM RELEASED BY WHICH BRITISH ROCK BAND IN 2019?

Q20: WHICH SINGER-SONGWRITER, ACTRESS AND AUTHOR HAD A HIT WITH SMILE IN 2006?

1960s-2000s

QUIZ

ANSWERS

WHICH OF YOU KNOWS THEIR POP MUSIC BEST?

1960s QUIZ 1 Answers

Q1 ANSWER: LIVERPOOL

Q2 ANSWER: MICK JAGGER

Q3 ANSWER: IT'S NOW OR NEVER

Q4 ANSWER: THUNDERBALL

Q5 ANSWER: DAVY JONES

Q6 ANSWER: JET PLANE

Q7 ANSWER: DUSTMAN

Q8 ANSWER: HAPPINESS

Q9 ANSWER: BIRMINGHAM

Q10 ANSWER: TOM JONES

1960s QUIZ 1 Answers

Q11 ANSWER: 1ST JANUARY 1964

Q12 ANSWER: ITSY BITSY TEENIE WEENIE YELLOW POLKADOT BIKINI

Q13 ANSWER: PINK FLOYD

Q14 ANSWER: ANYONE WHO HAD A HEART

Q15 ANSWER: WOODSTOCK

Q16 ANSWER: JIM MORRISON

Q17 ANSWER: THE MAMAS AND THE PAPAS

Q18 ANSWER: 17 NUMBER ONES

Q19 ANSWER: BLACK

Q20 ANSWER: DOLLY PARTON

1960s QUIZ 2
Answers

Q1 ANSWER: PAUL JONES '62-'66, MIKE D'ABO '66-'69

Q2 ANSWER: THE BEATLES

Q3 ANSWER: ERIC CLAPTON

Q4 ANSWER: GERRY AND THE PACEMAKERS

Q5 ANSWER: A WHITER SHADE OF PALE

Q6 ANSWER: THE SUPREMES

Q7 ANSWER: THE ANIMALS

Q8 ANSWER: THE BALAD OF JOHN AND YOKO 1969

Q9 ANSWER: LIVERPOOL

Q10 ANSWER: SGT PEPPER'S LONELY HEARTS CLUB BAND

1960s QUIZ 2 Answers

Q11 ANSWER: YOU – I REMEMBER YOU

Q12 ANSWER: 'IT'S NOT UNUSUAL' 1965 'THE GREEN GREEN GRASS OF HOME' 1966

Q13 ANSWER: THE SHADOWS

Q14 ANSWER: LULU

Q15 ANSWER: HOW MANY ROADS MUST A MAN WALK DOWN

Q16 ANSWER: THE CARNIVAL IS OVER

Q17 ANSWER: ENGELBERT HUMPERDINCK

Q18 ANSWER: PUPPET ON A STRING

Q19 ANSWER: THE ROLLING STONES

Q20 ANSWER: JIMI HENDRIX

1970s

QUIZ 1

Answers

Q1 ANSWER: RUPERT HOLMES

Q2 ANSWER: 1970

Q3 ANSWER: ERROL BROWN

Q4 ANSWER: THE MAN WITH THE GOLDEN GUN

Q5 ANSWER: THE BOYS ARE BACK IN TOWN

Q6 ANSWER: BRIDGE OVER TROUBLED WATER

Q7 ANSWER: SILVER LADY

Q8 ANSWER: DAVID BOWIE

Q9 ANSWER: 1979

Q10 ANSWER: 1974

Q11 ANSWER: STAYIN' ALIVE BY THE BEE GEES

Q12 ANSWER: THE MULL OF KINTYRE BY WINGS

Q13 ANSWER: LED ZEPPELIN

Q14 ANSWER: SATURDAY NIGHT FEVER

Q15 ANSWER: GARY NUMAN

Q16 ANSWER: SORRY - 'SORRY SEEMS TO BE THE HARDEST WORD' 1976

Q17 ANSWER: KC AND THE SUNSHINE BAND

Q18 ANSWER: GREASE

Q19 ANSWER: RUMOURS

Q20 ANSWER: ELECTRIC LIGHT ORCHESTRA

1970s QUIZ 2

Answers

Q1 ANSWER: TS ELIOT

Q2 ANSWER: KNOCK KNOCK WHO'S THERE?

Q3 ANSWER: PLAY THAT FUNKY MUSIC

Q4 ANSWER: THE CARPENTERS

Q5 ANSWER: NINE WEEKS

Q6 ANSWER: BYE BYE BABY

Q7 ANSWER: 1973

Q8 ANSWER: I CAN'T GIVE YOU ANYTHING (BUT MY LOVE)

Q9 ANSWER: 1978

Q10 ANSWER: BROTHERHOOD OF MAN

Q11 ANSWER: KIKI DEE

Q12 ANSWER: THE SPIDERS FROM MARS

Q13 ANSWER: CHILD – THE MAN WITH THE CHILD IN HIS EYES

Q14 ANSWER: WHAT'S GOING ON

Q15 ANSWER: MIKE OLDFIELD

Q16 ANSWER: KUNG FU – KUNG FU FIGHTING

Q17 ANSWER: AUSTRAILIA AND JAPAN

Q18 ANSWER: GEORGE HARRISON – MY SWEET LORD 1970

Q19 ANSWER: THE WURZELS

Q20 ANSWER: YOU'RE SO VAIN

1980s QUIZ 1 Answers

Q1 ANSWER: STATUS QUO

Q2 ANSWER: ALF

Q3 ANSWER: AC/DC

Q4 ANSWER: THE LIVING DAYLIGHTS

Q5 ANSWER: CORONATION STREET

Q6 ANSWER: RICK ASTLEY

Q7 ANSWER: 1985

Q8 ANSWER: PAUL YOUNG

Q9 ANSWER: AMERICA – LETTER FROM AMERICA

Q10 ANSWER: STAND AND DELIVER

1980s QUIZ 1 Answers

Q11 ANSWER: ST WINIFRED'S SCHOOL CHOIR

Q12 ANSWER: BANANARAMA

Q13 ANSWER: BUCKS FIZZ

Q14 ANSWER: BUSHY MEADS SECONDARY SCHOOL

Q15 ANSWER: U2

Q16 ANSWER: THE BREAKFAST CLUB

Q17 ANSWER: JOURNEY

Q18 ANSWER: THE RAINS

Q19 ANSWER: BONO

Q20 ANSWER: YAZZ

1980s QUIZ 2

Answers

Q1 ANSWER: EYE OF THE TIGER

Q2 ANSWER: KAJAGOOGOO (PROFESSIONAL NAME: LIMAHL)

Q3 ANSWER: PASS THE DUTCHIE

Q4 ANSWER: INTO THE GROOVE

Q5 ANSWER: 1983

Q6 ANSWER: NEIL TENNANT AND CHRIS LOWE

Q7 ANSWER: ANEKA

Q8 ANSWER: RESPECTABLE

Q9 ANSWER: GEORGE MICHAEL – I KNEW YOU WERE WAITING (FOR ME)

Q10 ANSWER: IT'S MY PARTY

Q11 ANSWER: DARWISH

Q12 ANSWER: ALWAYS ON MY MIND

Q13 ANSWER: THE SPECIALS

Q14 ANSWER: 1982

Q15 ANSWER: REGISTERED TRADEMARK FOR FOLLOW SPOTLIGHTS USED FOR STAGE EVENTS

Q16 ANSWER: CURIOSITY KILLED THE CAT

Q17 ANSWER: DON'T TURN AROUND

Q18 ANSWER: JOHN BONHAM

Q19 ANSWER: THE BEAUTIFUL SOUTH

Q20 ANSWER: I OWN YOU NOTHING

1990s QUIZ 1
Answers

Q1 ANSWER: PHIL DANIELS

Q2 ANSWER: BRITNEY SPEARS

Q3 ANSWER: (WHAT'S THE STORY) MORNING GLORY

Q4 ANSWER: HOWARD DONALD BORN 28/4/68

Q5 ANSWER: SUEDE

Q6 ANSWER: BITTER SWEET SYMPHONY

Q7 ANSWER: S CLUB 7

Q8 ANSWER: I'M BREATHLESS

Q9 ANSWER: 2994

Q10 ANSWER: REM

Q11 ANSWER: I WILL ALWAYS LOVE YOU

Q12 ANSWER: NEIGHBOURS

Q13 ANSWER: SINEAD O'CONNOR

Q14 ANSWER: THE STONE ROSES

Q15 ANSWER: 1990

Q16 ANSWER: ROBIN HOOD, PRINCE OF THIEVES

Q17 ANSWER: THE BEATLES

Q18 ANSWER: 1993

Q19 ANSWER: PEARL JAM

Q20 ANSWER: CREEP

1990s QUIZ 2 Answers

Q1 ANSWER: ABBA - ABBA-ESQUE

Q2 ANSWER: SIMPLY RED

Q3 ANSWER: 8 WEEKS

Q4 ANSWER: LOUISE - LOUISE GABRIELLE BOBB

Q5 ANSWER: 1998 - MAY

Q6 ANSWER: SATURDAY NIGHT

Q7 ANSWER: PRINCE

Q8 ANSWER: JARVIS COCKER

Q9 ANSWER: COUNTRY HOUSE

Q10 ANSWER: FREEDOM

1990s QUIZ 2 Answers

Q11 ANSWER: HAPPY MONDAYS

Q12 ANSWER: U2

Q13 ANSWER: DAVE NAVARRO

Q14 ANSWER: 1997

Q15 ANSWER: BELIEVE

Q16 ANSWER: AIN'T NO DOUBT

Q17 ANSWER: AQUA

Q18 ANSWER: KYLIE MINOGUE

Q19 ANSWER: JAMIROQUAI

Q20 ANSWER: FAT BOY SLIM

Q1 ANSWER: EVERGREEN

Q2 ANSWER: HALLELUJAH

Q3 ANSWER: UMBRELLA

Q4 ANSWER: LADY GAGA

Q5 ANSWER: DANGEROUSLY IN LOVE

Q6 ANSWER: WHERE IS THE LOVE?

Q7 ANSWER: EMINEM

Q8 ANSWER: MIKA

Q9 ANSWER: PARVA

Q10 ANSWER: FOLLOWILL

2000s QUIZ 1

<u>Answers</u>

Q11 ANSWER: 2006

Q12 ANSWER: SAM'S TOWN

Q13 ANSWER: OUR VERSION OF EVENTS

Q14 ANSWER: KATY PERRY

Q15 ANSWER: WESTLIFE

Q16 ANSWER: SHEFFIELD

Q17 ANSWER: JAY-Z

Q18 ANSWER: SNOOP DOGG

Q19 ANSWER: 2009

Q20 ANSWER: SIMPLY RED

2000s QUIZ 2

Answers

Q1 ANSWER: TAYLOR SWIFT

Q2 ANSWER: THE PROMISE

Q3 ANSWER: MCBUSTED

Q4 ANSWER: THINKING IT OVER

Q5 ANSWER: THE X FACTOR

Q6 ANSWER: THE PUSSYCAT DOLLS

Q7 ANSWER: 2006

Q8 ANSWER: SHAKIRA

Q9 ANSWER: NESSUN DORMA

Q10 ANSWER: RULE THE WORLD

2000s QUIZ 2

Answers

Q11 ANSWER: NICOLE KIDMAN

Q12 ANSWER: MEL C - MELANIE CHISHOLM

Q13 ANSWER: CHAIN REACTION

Q14 ANSWER: OOPS!...I DID IT AGAIN

Q15 ANSWER: IT WON'T BE SOON BEFORE LONG

Q16 ANSWER: LITTLE MIX

Q17 ANSWER: KYLIE MINOGUE

Q18 ANSWER: FRANZ FERDINAND

Q19 ANSWER: COLD PLAY

Q20 ANSWER: LILY ALLEN

THANK YOU!

Thank you for buying this book. I hope it has given you and your family and friends some fun!

If you would like to see the rest of the books in my Princetown Books range, you will find them by scanning the QR Code below or by putting bit.ly/PRINCETOWNBOOKS into your browser's search bar 🩶

Printed in Great Britain
by Amazon

50403011R00050